Selected Poems

Previous publications by Peter Hughes

The Interior Designer's Late Morning, Many Press 1983
Bar Magenta (with Simon Marsh), Many Press, 1986
Odes on St. Cecilia's Day, Poetical Histories, 1990
The Metro Poems, Many Press, 1992
Psyche in the Gargano, Equipage, 1995
Paul Klee's Diary, Equipage, 1995
Keith Tippet Plays Tonight, Maquette Press, 1999
Blueroads: Selected Poems, Salt Publishing, 2003
Sound Signals Advising of Presence, infernal methods, 2006
Minor Yours, Oystercatcher Press, 2006
Nistanimera, Shearsman Books, 2007
The Sardine Tree, Oystercatcher, 2008
The Summer of Agios Dimitrios, Shearsman, 2009
Behoven, Oystercatcher, 2009
The Pistol Tree Poems (with Simon Marsh), Shearsman, 2011
Interscriptions (with John Hall), Knives Forks And Spoons Press, 2011
Regulation Cascade, Oystercatcher, 2012
Soft Rush, Red Ceilings Press, 2013
Quite Frankly, Like This Press, 2013

Selected Poems

Peter Hughes

Shearsman Books

First published in the United Kingdom in 2013 by
Shearsman Books
50 Westons Hill Drive
Emersons Green
BRISTOL
BS16 7DF

Shearsman Books Ltd Registered Office
30–31 St. James Place, Mangotsfield, Bristol BS16 9JB
(this address not for correspondence)

www.shearsman.com

ISBN 978-1-84861-271-6

Copyright © Peter Hughes, 2013.

The right of Peter Hughes to be identified as the author
of this work has been asserted by him in accordance with the
Copyrights, Designs and Patents Act of 1988.
All rights reserved.

Acknowledgements

The poems in this volume previously appeared in the following publications.
Thanks to the editors and publishers concerned.

Active in Airtime, Angel Exhaust, Beard of Bees, Cambridge Literary Review, Chapman, Constant Red/Mingled Damask, The Cutting Room, *Ekleksographia, Exultations & Difficulties, Fine Madness, Fire, First Offense, Folded Sheets, Fragmente, Gairfish, Geometer,* The Gig, Great Works, Intercapillary Space, Numinous Magazine, Orbis, Outposts, Pivot, Poetry Wales, Ramraid Extraordinaire, Sunk Island Review, Shadow Train, Stimulus Response, Tears in the Fence, *10th Muse,* Terrible Work, Tremblestone, Unarmed Journal, Upstairs at Duroc, Verse, West Coast Magazine.

Bar Magenta (with Simon Marsh; Many Press), *Odes on St. Cecilia's Day* (Poetical Histories), The Metro Poems (Many Press), *Paul Klee's Diary* (Equipage), *Psyche in the Gargano* (Equipage), *Blueroads* (Salt Publishing), *Sound Signals Advising of Presence* (infernal methods), *Nistanimera* (Shearsman Books), *The Sardine Tree* (Oystercatcher), *The Summer of Agios Dimitrios* (Shearsman), *Lynn Deeps* (Red Ceilings), *18* (Knives Forks & Spoons Press), *An Unofficial Roy Fisher* (Shearsman), *Behoven* (Oystercatcher), *Interscriptions* (with John Hall; Knives Forks & Spoons Press), *The Pistol Tree Poems* (with Simon Marsh; Shearsman), *Sabi* (Crater), *Site Guide* (The Arthur Shilling Press), *Collected Letters* (Wild Honey), *Allotment Architecture* (Reality Street).

Contents

Ars Poetica	9
Premonition	10
The Seasons	11
Ode on St. Cecilia's Day	17
from The Metro Poems	
Ottaviano	22
Spagna	22
Repubblica	23
Manzoni	24
S. Giovanni	25
Ponte Lungo	26
Furio Camillo	26
Lucio Sestio	27
Giulio Agricola	27
Subaugusta	28
Colosseo	29
Piramide	30
Magliana	31
Marconi	31
Fermi	32
Laurentina	32
Quintet for St. Cecilia's Day	33
Education Policy	36
Apples	37
Night Driving	38
Psyche in the Gargano	39
from Paul Klee's Diary	43
West Coast	58
Tenor Legacy	58
Joe Pass Live in Every Hedge	59
Real Book	59
Oystercatcher	60
Starfish	62
Landing	63
from The Green Hill	64

Peg	64
Liederkreis	65
from The Summer of Agios Dimitrios	68
from The Pistol Tree Poems	83
from Lynn Deeps	108
Poly-Olbion	111
from Behoven	112
Sabi	127
from Collected Letters	129
from Site Guide	136
from 18	139
from Interscriptions	141
from Quite Frankly	143
from The Sardine Tree	145

for Lynn

Ars Poetica

Sooner or later
on the cold and parching landing
where the clock hands unravel
the golf-ball innards of your head
a telephone rings in a room
to which you've lost the keys.

A granular waggling
as of sand and a flounder's tail
is the vestigial soul
which flaps up from its bed
as you shoulder the door crashing
into vacant sunlit space

where the phone has stopped.
In front of the window
a plastic bag of water turns
suspended from the pelmet
and fans the lunchtime light
in gold and marching bars across your face.

Premonition

A bee trudges through the air behind me
appears and charges the pink swing doors
of a moist and odorous June rose.
Trees hold creosoted plates where lopped
phantom branches once grew. The noise
of crows and a mower stops behind the fence.
To understand the elevation of silence
you would want to go through the last tick
of the mower, the big square of sun
on planks, the stink of damp mint
and old splintering timber. Exactly then
you see that the perfect circle opposite
wasn't a hard black knot in the wood
but a hole into the neighbours' dark premises.

The Seasons

i

Night squats to listen as the boiler
starts playing chanter to the local dogs.
Metaphors trundle up the garden path
like bison on roller skates
ignoring the shuttered windows
encased in scaly plaster.

I believe in nights remains inscribed
beneath this heavy souvenir ashtray
with burnt butts resting at the brim,
stocky doubled-up sailors asleep on the moon.

What was the name of that film?

Drawn through perfectly empty pages,
clean pulls to the mind's beach,
that gargling surf which darkened
behind the retina like toast

O those were not the days
when the tilted world leaked
legends of the seasons into my glass

colossal life-guards in wheel-chairs.

The very next day we threw
crusts into our lapping faces
from the top of Rainbow Bridge.
You were saying someone had forgotten
to wind up the mallards and swans
when, daft as a grebe's tuft,
Spring unbuttoned its wet mac.

ii

I'd swim upstream, thump my tail on the stones,
sliver over meadows in a black tube,
chew out a nest 'neath whichever eaves you pleased

it's that look in your eyes which
licks the sky's cake-bowl clean
turning fathoms of light
riding through the west windows
galloping up your spine
trotting through your hair
rearing under your wrists
shaken like manes by your coming

to reassemble as the lulled pool
of your breath and disappear in sleep.

The afternoon seeps away behind
venetian blinds to the diminishing
squeak of little wheels.

Evenings are so much longer.

iii

In Summer shirts get dirtier sooner
to be washed in grandmother's shampoo.
Sun leans on the brick bell towers,
bags of cement lean on the old hives.

Territorial traffic noses and barges
past faulty traffic-lights where you haul
on your carrier-bags which won't last out,
ubiquitous stretch marks dangerously
transparent between the handle and name.

They all make out your scantily clad aubergines
as the bus creates merry hell over stopping.

The white terrier squats on the dusty verge
uneasily turning her head as the metro
soars beneath her away from the centre.

I was hanging out my washing on the terrace
admiring the dusk plants sprouting from the church roof
when I turned as you switched on the lights.
You were laughing in the kitchen but I like
splashing about in suds and Marzemino then
pegging up my green check shirt under the moon.

So if I wake up a bit under the weather
my shirt's already up and about
flapping its arms through the window
beckoning towards impossible directions.

iv

My birthday's in the Autumn
so I get a new and bigger rucksack.
Hiding the past and future
among my favourite books and jumpers
I swing the present onto my shoulder.
The left strap gives way.

The season leaches out through mulch
and post offices where every day
is a blocked culvert under the few
passing cars that drench the hedges,
popping premature chestnuts
from their rotting cream head gear.
The curtains are parted by dawn.

Dew and new mushrooms glimmer by garden trees—
matted, tended surfaces penetrated by cold stalks
shedding spore white in the postman's footprint.
You tidied laundry, pens and hair
turned toast, eggs and pages balancing
October light on the inside of your wrist.

The alder bronzed in the last of evening
its boughs rose on the darkening wind.
The water edge sounded through soaked gravel
below each separate leaf, minutes from
the beginning or end of all vespers.

Vespers! the very word recalls the second hand
scooter that carries you to your temporary
bar job where in fifteen minutes you'll
unwrap and test the Guinness tap.

v

My warmed up roll had the Union Jack
on a stick stuck in it. Affecting
to assemble snugly ham and tomatoes
it really merely held the cheery
rectangle and formed an occupied hole.

Then as I considered everything
that didn't grow and your green
tights it stabbed me in the gum.

Fortunately, a couple of pounds
of petrol will carry you up
from this dank and uppity plain
to the mountains' crisp vacuity.

Up from baffled voices, trodden
echoes in crescents and back streets

past sheep like clotted mist
to the hiss and click of skis
that slip over buried fences.

Our grins blue with postponement
we wobble back from the sunset
where all definitions lie
under the tracks we make and follow.

Slovenly beauties of effort and release,
our tracks upon the world
harden out there for a few days
as we sit back from the fire
borrowed dust and ice in our turn ups.

vi

Down we drift on the great ship
fishing, launching kites, performing
Punch and Judy for the crew.
We saw the glimmer of discarded ring-pulls
out of the corners of our eyes
as marvellous fish culminating
in the circle of achieved possibility.

I see the porthole in the mirror
as I shave and make the air hum
like canvas under Morandi vases.
The reason for being here
is to preclude the question and poetry
looking forwards over your own shoulder.

Another show has finished in the tiny
planetarium where nothing has set,
not even the nicely formed concavity
where you leant in my presence.

A float punctures the river's sheen
the line looped and acock.
A sideways nudge frees the water.
The weighted float sits straight and deep
its luminous tip fitting the slow current.

A paper sounding-board
beats in the rhythm of the air.
You don't know which is your pulse
which the pluck of the kite
as the winds take you by the hand
then take your breath away.

Ode on St. Cecilia's Day

1
Baggy old whores topple by in perms,
dust trickling down the back of the day
           on a sudden runnel of sweat
as a slovenly Trastevere afternoon yawns,
scratches its crotch and listlessly slags off the neighbours.
Further grumbling at the doorstep of the head
           is the pronged scoop of a JCB
either scraping the street clean or dragging
the surface into unnavigable ruts.
Well below this sour pillow and its load,
a train smelling of the dead approaches
a Metro station which has been filled in
with weeds, lens caps, ketchup, mud and rubble.
That ringing thump is the last level and trace
being slapped flat with the back of a shovel.

2
He said, Cecily, something about a typical afternoon.
An ant in a rubber glove could've said as much
           without such suppository-smugness.
Odd words in green script do indeed traverse
VDUs on western cliffs, while rusty speakers
croak out compositions of static and fear.
An entire day had again gone unrecognised
in distant rumours of the ring-road,
a last draughty sun, weeds' shadows lengthening.
From the direction of the Aventine,
below the nasal nocturne of the shawm—
hark! a sackbut, in the Mixolydian mode,
on a Travertine dunlopillow of 'cellos.

3
Curve of revenge,
a sniff,
the racket
of a brimming galvanised bucket
        crashing on the marble
                stopping dead
                      nothing spilt

ripples chasing each other
into their vacant hearts.

4
Through a lurid night of sticky dreams
this pillow of lace, Marmite smears and ooze
bobs above a rising sea-horse,
pouch crammed and wriggling,
continuing his tilted ascent forwards
the swaying ocean's moony roof

November exhales a lunar tastelessness
in owls' quiet hoops of sound
and dry leaves settling on dry stone.

She is only in the trappings of the world,
her musics staving off the night.

5
The dripping stops as a dense steam
unfurls along the hall.
In a zone of suffocation the sun
        has gnawed out its heart.
Night wades in the full moon of the piazza
where thirst and senses have been quenched
in the last days of the grape harvest.

Between imploded hangover and distant alarm-clocks
mounds of grapes sail past the moist hedge of dawn
where the god sits with an erection like a tow bar.
At sunrise it's even harder to overlook debt
or hard-boiled egg on the harp strings.

6
A couple of cells like notes
              have knitted fire into time.
We come in waves and particles too
beyond the comedies of measurement,
night ending in a bunched tangle of sonorous
              cocks and bells.
In a dream full of steam, blades and
              plunging consummation,
her pulse beat against the sheet
in the hollow beneath her ankle.
An absence at the edge of the lane
is an idea which began to be relished
beyond the shimmering flute arabesque
or the laborious dirge of the organ.

7
A rower stirs tree reflection,
sliding down the bloated khaki Tiber.
Frayed bunting dangles overhead and the stretch
between the bridges is empty again.

              I underestimated more than you can say.

Way downstream the oarsman is making
a pig's ear out of a silken curve—
changing his own notions of space.
              Her sleeping statue's hand hangs
              over the edge of the niche.

Later there's this garlicky panoply:
brilliant awning taut over
           a cerise and charcoal accordion,
the saxophone's brazen belly-landing,
the splash and ripples of the cymbals.
A string bass walks over our graves
as we chew bits of space and pizza.

8
           This line is made of air,
bees browsing dusty chicory and thistle,
traffic and impulse clotting along the Appia.
Dead weeds scrape in the breeze
under power lines that swoop towards Rome.
Helicopters return low over eastern beaches,
the tough and legendary headlands
of another black and white video.
Meanwhile we screw up our faces,
           plug guitars into the wind
as the knots of interference extend down
through money, vowel and memory
to the new veins and ore of the Earth
(that kicked, delicious, recolonised skull of God).

9
Lizards slip into cracks under broken glass,
ants' nests and blackened pork bones.
The gypsies have deserted the meadow which gapes
between the rind in the weeds and wind in the reeds.
           Embraced by the final sphere,
each movement spurts streams of enharmonic atoms
which, so they said, popped up in the bedroom too
once every twenty million years or so.
Galaxies pack their bags—new neighbours move in.

        In her final silent cavatina
she had tried to sing the rate of creation in a sphere
of radius ten to the power nine light years
        in tons per second.
She sang of water on the stem
and she sang of human want
as a vast black matted ball
that could be coughed up from a cat's throat.

from The Metro Poems

Ottaviano

> For Art Pepper

A plush satin bag of tumbly pumice
You could practically hold with your toes.
Under careering petrel and plummeting gannet,
Hiccoughing whales and tamarisk seaweed
Salute unstacked fathoms of departing tide.
Bivalves clap too slowly as mermaids' purses
Roll down the slopes of irregular beds
Through softly abrasive sand and shingle
In restless attempts to succour the alto line.
Unexpended waves lisp along the beaches
To where tangy spit dances on a reed
At the margins of desolate headlands.
Town is a plane tree singing in night wind
Shadowing the steps to the underground.

Spagna

      I'm raining on shadows
you're crammed as a pie
loaded with ore and yellow curd
Mercury dissolves one grain
sugar on the ironed tarpaulin
my bag smells of coconut oil
in the bag it's still night
      watery-coloured sea
harmonica damp with brown ale
Uncle William flushed considering

Birmingham firmament
        Windscreen smashed
        radio stolen
something nameless
still whispering
        through the speakers
dawn and her down treading
deftly lightly slightly
like joy over the lobes
Niels Bohr said   It's
        wrong to think
        the task of physics
        is to find out
        how nature is.
        Physics concerns
        what we can
        say about nature.

Repubblica

For Tom Hughes

An uneasy combination of Sardinian wine
and Venus has risen over the petrol station.
Patterns of suburban shadows stretch away
under the brightness of the Pleiades,
between the dark continents of cloud that merge
in the time it takes to smoke a cigarette.

Somewhere a politician is looking up 'bayonetting'
to see if it's spelt with one t or two.
Somewhere a priest is studying results
of recent municipal elections.
The baby sleeps through the subsequent storm

among prints of elephants and penguins
while lousy bright-eyed dogs over the road
hunch between chained gates and lightning.

On the morning after the boy's birth
the church's grubby window illuminated
two gas cylinders tucked under the altar
and steps leading down to a dank, rectangular absence.
When the talk turns to baptism, I see the child
a thousand feet higher—a river flowing through
burnished ironstone pebbles and steep forest.
The river Sangro, twenty five paces wide,
shallow as water poured over the hands,
where they say wolves still come to drink at night.

Manzoni

These two soft washed blisters, unconnected
and awry on an outstretched hand,
make you think of how a sickle is held.
Only the plum tree has survived this worn
thin blade, slimy with sap, that's toppled nettles,
smacked through dock, flowerpots and rhubarb,
pulling bindweed wriggling from the roses.
The old tree's all massy and misshapen,
too hacked about then too long neglected—
a great lolling freight of top-heaviness.
All we can do now is savour the fruit
as straining branches bow to the present,
the only place we're ever going to live,
never really learning to call it home.

S. Giovanni

The theft of the next breath out of the air
seems tricky and precipitous, each mouthful
tasting of panicky evacuation.
The pulse shoots out of the ventricle fast,
like a stolen Ford from an underground car-park.
Under the perhaps contemporary stars
the mind empties in anticipation and sends
a rippling glow treading and dancing
                              fading over the core.
The day painting stopped was a chasm
yawned under an ambulance
blocked in a clutter of rush-hour traffic.
The unnerving evening slouched under a window
thrown open high in the Vatican Palace
to the distant strains of 'Tracks of my Tears'
by Smokey Robinson and the Miracles.
Traffic extended beyond every sense
to a dark incantation of night rain
fluttering up through strangers' headlights.
At the end, when the visitors had gone,
sun edged along the walls discovering
the broad brush strokes of the finished fresco.
Rooms of poised, horizontal light echoed a light
withdrawing footfall and half-remembered muttering.
A last watcher, clairaudient and delayed,
traced the interwoven forms in the wall
standing up to her neck in shadow.
Evening light was saying the art is
also to work fast on drying plaster.

Ponte Lungo

The winter lake still hasn't frozen.
Through dark branches of pathside hornbeam
a hundred golden persimmon beat
on a slope of dusk and hillside wind.
Each fruit hangs, a Chinese lantern,
vulnerable and desirable as next year's songs.
The path crosses a stream whose icy clarity
plucks dregs spiralling into the lake
like words dancing into oblivion.
For a moment, from this angle,
the waters grow luminous. Another step
and constellations sway by your feet.

Furio Camillo

The first figs have split at the seams
in the famously endless Roman night.

She briefly rippled across
the darkened windows of shops and cafes

vacant words tracing and echoing steps.

Within the jerky circlings of bats,
crickets' tetchy scratchings complement
the far harmonics of mid-Summer stars.

Sleepless, a neighbour
is murmuring to some god or child.

Lucio Sestio
> For Peter Riley

June trees rock breathless in sap and frill.
Slipstream from an invisible wing brushes
Eyelashes as the stomach grasps the erosive
Stone of the years. Cold space within each name
Untouched by Tuscan sun, wind of sage and thyme
Waving yellows of gorse and broom. The space
Seems inaccessible, neglected for decades
Though tucked beneath the heart's full cistern.
Listen to the drip: leakage from the current
Forming tiny channels which will flood and dissolve
Into the estuary of your remotest breaths.
Among these present branchings, parted foliage
Of the self drops light down towards potential
Growth you can barely imagine, and offer.

Giulio Agricola
> for Simon's birthday

This morning your brain will stir, wake, lose hold
    Like a biscuit dunked in the irresistibility of all those
Dotted 'I's, Kandinsky interjections beeped inside eyelids.
    Still life, natura morta, 1960, Milan, private collection.
Five white beakers next to a crock of rough red wine
    Big as a bubble-car. On such an evening,
Settling down to bonsai a new balcony poem,
    The balcony is a fat basket swung under the flappy balloon
Of the night—see how it sails away! feel how it bumps
    And nuzzles the roof-tops! I'm perfectly aware that morning
Does crash into your head like a small red vehicle,
    The balcony strangely beached on the side of the building,
Mind stuck on the sharp stick of the spine. By now

    You're gingerly enclosed in morning as the queue outside
The astrologer's grows like amoeba making elbow room.
    Shopping we can usually handle—I'll have two trees
And that monkfish please. Wet broad beans have invaded the district,
    Clods of sheep-cheese obliterate the weather forecast.
Giulio Agricola is ankle deep in cacky over-ripe courgette goo
    And you're struck that it's always sunrise on the Earth.
Houses preen their tiles, air their gaps in the day.
    Puddles go to heaven feet first—suddenly it's evening.
Streets in cinemascope, the spirit a parachute for the sun
    Whose upstreams fuse certain April notations
Onto the balcony trellis. You regard this rum pattern,
Swallow, tend the new ring in your trunk.

Subaugusta
    For St. Cecilia's Day

    On the marble tables of Bar Magenta
You empty out keys, coin and azure plectra
    Sequacious of the lyre and spinach sandwiches.
Traffic rounds up head-tapping pigeons
    To the rapt encouragement of Japanese circuitry
Headphones twitching pinching brains.
    In the music room squat the black boxes
Intensive care wiring sprouting forth.
    These are the kennels of spirits,
Pretty maids all in a rowdy pillow fight
    Stopping, hardly even giggling, when we peep.

    As the storm seeped out of your plimsolls
Your feet felt the world a stage
    Where very few hold an Equity Card.
That back alley rhythm like Chaplin's walk
    Bends notes so far up they go right off

The neck, and you're percussive, fretting air.
        Ever since Mum told you Dad was the dragon god
You've been stroked and constricted by coils
        Jangling up through the scales to the open
Balcony windows where you chuck down buckets of
        Glistening notes onto these dull peripheries.

        Hand over your longest chords of wire
Wool, juice and impasto. Don't wipe your
        Large and jumbled footprints off the air.
There's more space outside, and in.
        Forgetting our keys and selves
We can clamber up all seven floors
        To the music room where tall and sourceless
Shadows career and brightly bob
        To trampolines of song that launch us
On whippy parabolas to crunchy hangover
        Breakfasts and music shall untune the sky.

Colosseo

        The next evictions take place tomorrow,
a gas fire eating the dust of summer
        between spare blue buds and a reddening grill.
The sister he nursed until death, through months
        ridden with disease, unease and priests
finally left the world and flat to the church.
        He casts listlessly from the island in the Tiber
watching without quite seeing the varnished quill
        lean upstream and edge into a backwater.
A year's gone by and still the odd letter
        turns up addressed to no-one, August brushing
mass upon mass of fig, nettle and elder.
        Every evening he waits for it to get dark

as young tench—the little doctor fish—
       amble around the bright unbaited hook.
On his last morning there he pottered out
       in slippers past the church where organist
and bride were tottering into a beautifully rickety
       Ode to Joy; where resplendent frescoed angels
gaze and punt befuddled sinners through an
       unseen crack in the bricked-up gates of hell.

Piramide

This is where the Metro meets the coast train,
rumbling the tanned and sandy underground
where our vulnerability itches,
invisible insects wrapped in damp towels.
Beyond the evening terminus, wind is
filling absence, neither cleansing nor erosive.
The audible music seems to have stopped;
sea pours from bottles swung out from the surf,
reflections sparkling in the barging tides.
Attending her footprints that counterpoint
the far gleaming boom of memory's shoreline,
hearing her endless paddling through night's breakers,
the fact remains we arrive and will leave
along a quiet road by a beach at night.

Magliana

Knees and cheekbones, temptations to tamper
with skeletons and whatnot in her cupboard.
Precipitations just dust the outlines
on this meringuey morning, eyebrow cocked
over a 1968 Keep up your Italian.
But from the dewy, filthy train for Magliana
I headed for the bridge, missed, waded in and
down the bed, bubbling, treading aquatic veg.
Craning up to the wobbling light I periscoped
a finger to wiggle a feel of the sun.
Dripping up the other bank, shedding weed and gudgeon
I held the melted night tightly aloft—
O how she'd plucked, revolved, doused down
and scoured the gristly cockles of my heart.

Marconi

Fascist graffiti caress Fascist walls
at the end of the Infernetto road,
the site of the Easter bonfire already
ringed with waist-high grasses dribbling seed.
Mosquitoes flit across unexorcised ground
as wine is shared by the angular lake
where nightingale song can sometimes be heard
way below the fertile constellations.
La religione del mio tempo
rests next to the cold water and cold wine
and nightingale song is a physical shock
as grasses mutter seed into the wind.
We are never going to see the light
threshed tonight in the courtyards of the stars.

Fermi

It is of no consequence
that wherever a bus-stop sign
is wrenched out of the path
and chucked over a hedge

some priest with new sandals
horny toe-nails and a gold tooth
climbs the gate, wades the wet grass
and waits for the 47.

Laurentina

A dream of buds nudging the brain's crust
in a greenish luminous night of spring,
the raw blare of Arcturus, intimate and alien
as a stomach ulcer or disused urban canal.
Among cool, unheard movements of dark gardens
first apple blossom is as still as the night
before the moon goes back beneath the hills.
Top branches move in a breath of sunrise
spilling petals, signalling another
human dawn paling into significance.

A wicker basket lined with dust and muslin
stands on the living room table.
Greengages, masonry nails and copper washers
arbitrarily nestle inside.
Nor could we plan the love that like
light billows irregularly into the room
where we are continuously banished
through the edges of fingers and voices
towards the sky's insubstantial consonance.

Quintet for St. Cecilia's Day

1

Bells begin, then others, then a third peal lacing
much of morning with drips
from the sleeves of an old white shirt—
water seeping along the interstices of terrace tiles.

A sleeve, yellow plastic peg and endless sky
are perfectly reflected in a shrinking puddle
until sun is back on baked, unreflective clay.

Consciousness is at least this precarious
as the Summer night opens around
the triangle of Deneb, Altan, Vega.

2

I don't think any significant distances have been covered
since the landlord traipsed by with servant and bandy gait
a couple of days or weeks or centuries ago.
Money sits in the back of the car behind tinted windows
dark glasses and conditioned air.
Arranged in the boot are the usual accoutrements:
leather briefcase, heavy stick, tapes of sentimental songs.
As lightning splits and plummets like a mining accident,
there are certain clarities
which no one can mistake for simplification.
Life has embraced us like a Sumo wrestler to whom we submit
whilst affecting to raise it up before our faces
between the tips of our fingers.

3

She breathes into her hand as the plums hang and soften,
expressionless while a refreshing draught plays around ribs
and acidic memories of a chipped, discarded mirror.
Discovered in a hedge of childhood, its flaking silver
showed young nettles where her eyes would have been,
hair pouring through too much sky.
On a nearby site, of nettles and riverside light,
a willow grew through each year's pollarding—
when she was born a birch seed nestled in the willow crotch,
cracked and budded in the shoulder-high damp lap.
I think some dryad spread her insistencies
down through the hollow host and up among its branches
till a wrist-thick root dressed in birch bark
handled the earth of the river bank as its own.

4

This wine tastes of pears and cunnilingus
as the island stands in deep green seas
waving absence, broom and asphodels.

This shudder on the tape is where I walked
across bare floor-boards, recording her music,
to the bed where the pulse stove in the brain.

Even before the boyish employees turned up
to crow-bar the door from its frame,
posing around flimsy fistwork
mimicked from fictitious childhood heroes,

she had tasted the tastelessness of the sacrificial—
the belching vacuities of violence and worlds well lost.
By then her only mirrors were orchard windows,
irregularities of Autumn light on the ceilings of the house.

5

Light fails for the first stars
beyond the warm muck of the horizons.
Throughout the long night
radio music is interspersed with assurances
of election, peace and justice.

Standing below the slow flight of Cygnus
and the imperceptible progress of Pegasus,
she sensed the vowels and dangerous beauty of Cassiopeia
rhyme with the goose-flesh of November.

In the cold, iron-eyed hours before dawn
I have heard her padding into the living room
to open a window into the thunder.

Education Policy

Don't talk to individuals or small groups much less
    let them learn to talk to each other. Stand at the
front—watch the exits. Maintain standards on gold
    sticks someone has to fail it must be people
people who should populate the margins so privilege
    can dig deeper and deeper until one day it may
bore right through the core of the Earth with its
    pockets full of pips and roughage then an edible
eviscerated core can bask in the cosy oven of certain
    of our fathers' heavens. Write poetry about hedges
or copy out poems about hedges to discipline script
    there is only one correct way to write not leaving
any space between an m and a p—insist on these bonds
    they determine success and cohesion. With luck
the successful will subsist on their memory of success
    until impotent, while the unsuccessful will be able
to subsist for decades on a deep sense of release from
    schizoid desolation. Teach in Subject. Keep History,
Language, Education for Citizenship distinct: preclude
overview and connection. Learning by heart means
    memorising the unexamined: only the memorising
is subject to examination. It should never be
    learning by heart which is a figure of speech
whose implications don't bare examination. Thank you.

Apples

That light between finger-tip size apples
is the gassy haze of Jupiter
on remote fences of Virgo.
Most of my ideas are back in the house
in an upstairs room behind windows
inside a scuffed leather briefcase.
I forgot to turn off the tape-recorder
after speaking and now summer night
winds silently onto the spool.
At this end of the garden I wouldn't hear
the click as the tape goes taut
effecting the next transformation.
A lifetime later, premonitions of dawn
whisper around the house's silhouette,
the early brilliance of Venus,
and children who sleep into day
with the comfort of a small night-light.

Night Driving

All the miles and nights I drove
    forcing thought back under the wheels
(mid-mornings curled up on back seats
    in some lay-by, rocked, buffeted
with litter and leaves
    by passing cars and trucks)—
I can't touch a road now without
    that spot seeming to be the centre
of one of those great night journeys
    to nowhere in particular
just maximum distance stuffed into
    the nocturnal sack of the self.
Even when asleep I find myself
    pulling out to overtake a dream
glancing up to a dark mirror
    right foot testing the weight of covers.
At night the warm tyres spin
    among the comments of the dead
while the road caresses
    and smoothes down the depth of tread.

Psyche in the Gargano

1

Lighter beer is best for mornings
of blue vacancy too insubstantial to savour—
not even the topmost eucalyptus leaves move
as the sea breathes in weed and recumbency
swaying under the Psychozoic age's freight.
       Like many DIY fumes this scenery
       is raw gnawing at the tonsils,
smouldering down and you know the way
the solar plexus goes up like touchpaper
when leant to Nature's affections
and there's no doubt at all in your head
because there's nothing at all in your head,
just early stellar emotions that sherbet
the marrow, muddy the blood, warm the fat
of the palm where a little gilded smear
is the farthest word, or last jelly tot.
       The fields of love and dream
       slope down beyond the pale.
But as soon as it starts tipping its white hats,
seething the beaches, olive trees
winking, pinching themselves all over,
no-one's breeze handling the Aleppo pines
       then a beaker of cool Cioccarello
       with its bright, specific power
       better relates afternoon plans
to their absence from forthcoming decades.
I expect life started here too, gravid currents
easing up from darker beds, slipping into
flip-flops, shuffling through summery berm.
All the water's draining out of my think-tank
       but I do like the way plants eat light
then we eat them, and all this gristly, airy business.
       She is sense edging past in the shadows

        to rumours of a wide withdrawing tide
        that rocks below a low and open moon.
She becomes a tree and hut in karst country
stiffening among spectacular drinks
within the luminous tickle of aeolation—
        lids and lintels decked in crystals
        standing out below the Northern Cross.
        She's encrusted with knobbly cones and salt
whispering needles down onto the roof's corrugations,
a gasping face beneath you in the dark.

2

The drunk dumped up in the crow's nest
was shouting at dawn again this morning
as we cracked the last tin of dried biscuit,
scooped bright scum from the water cask.
Dazed with the sway of undulating months
our lightning printed pain on the timbers
while depression clotted to a rotten milk.
Dawn wind brought strange herbs on deck
where once we almost recognised ourselves,
        memory and resentment melting
        in the delicious creak and tautening
        that tugged our sails into
        paunches you could play upon with drum-sticks,
        spume cast dancing back along the sea.
Under the wondering words of the ocean
hidden tons of sea-light flex and settle
the measure of our poise and restlessness.
You row against estuary thrust,
joyously punch the damp sand of some homeland.
You always think to go further on in,
deeper into the interior towards heartland
and it is better to think in such a way
for hearts cave in, wet cardboard boxes,

at the sight of our camping in salt-wind,
flysheets spread like lichens
on limestone terraces, social tundra
and the night's reckless exposures.
Morning rolls us up the paths of the sun—
        a hill reaching into the wind,
        one rough, tortuous track
        worn on its massive sour shoulder.
The valley course is obscured
in haze and a comfort of woodsmoke.
Stone, overgrown, clutched by oak,
hints at ancient civic edges where breeze
        falls into a theatre
        of monumental echoing steps
a cupped hand of rock holding sun-drizzle
light and silence while the dog dives
after a lizard, whines pawing at brambles,
disappears into the hill.

3

You don't decide at the end of which twig
you emerge like a trembling drop of dew,
suspended over the endless winking lawns
where sea-winds sway through rain and tamarisk
and the swiftly flowing winter Thames
flowed and flew through bright discomfort,
sparrows' skirts blown up around their necks
wind picking sleet and forsythia from the
prospect of a pleasure boat pulling past
its load of old diesel and tinsel.
Over English breakfast of aspirin and tea
stars bellow across domestic horizons
birch, apple and holly burn
from the eye corner procession edges
chocolate weeks, song and bitterness

the acrid finds of adolescence
newts and marsh marigolds
moss lanes, shadow and vetch-green
Paschal cakes, pallid wicks, charred aubade
        pulling the skin back
        tenderly touching up
        waiting is dying
        hissing with relief
        shouting into the coal-hole
        cider-breath luxury
mist squinting in at knowledge.
The dark growls at a bark from the south
tips back her head and barks north as
the restaurant dogs take it up
toss it on to leap and insinuate
from Scylla, Charybdis, peaked hut
darkened forest and windless seas
the old blue caravan under sunset
        here in the sultry rancid clearing
        here in the cluttered whispering desert
        here on the lucid sands of Mudeford
        here on the choked high-tide of Annet
        here in the tasted fog of Galway Bay
factory gates opening at evening
great formations of bikes and mopeds
flowing through the deepening
streets between the darkening
houses, yards and heavens of Cowley
from all the undone Sicilian nights
to the blue and slushy heart of Russia
the breath in neighbouring kitchens.

from Paul Klee's Diary

1

I made you up
I called you Eveline
my lady of the bright patch
virgin on the imponderable

squirming
on the bright hook of the ideal

as a child
I thought rollmop herrings
were The Beatles

& the maid's genitals
a clump of four willies
arranged like an udder

when just the two of us
were left alone
I used to squat on the head of the broom
while she pushed & pulled
till I'd ridden the whole floor

covering every forgotten
absent
or anticipated footfall

consciousness was nuzzled
camouflaged & stitched up
by the patchwork landscapes
of every aquarium owner in the west

certain deaths sprout deep in the skull
it's just a way of doing up your shirt

down here in the hold
icy black sea is nearer your heart
than are your hands

when you lie down
it talks about your body

sleep caked with red salt
a menagerie of demons squinted
through the crystals

daft boys next door whispered
God was always watching us

fish were always watching me

according to mother
I'll never wear
ravishing lace-trimmed white panties
as after only four years
I'm to be a boy forever

it's an interesting phase

then the boys consider Mrs Berg
older that a cellar and dead
hush!
she's turning into an angel
imagine

to go with his big pallid knobbly ball of a brain
the lad next door was probably born
with cauliflower ears

I think
angels make good pictures

my lady of the damp patch
Camille of the pale red dress

sleep was guarded by crumbling
columns of grey salt
twisted wet papers arched in the bin

midnight chimed from desolation
all the way to Berlin & back again

I am back where I awoke
to a dark state studded with fireflies
further than the eye could see

come home—talk about defective verbs

whenever I get a squall in the head
or vertigo while standing on the ground

I feel tons of water moving sideways beneath me
slippy with misplaced herring that wag
against the current in order to stay & watch
Camille walk backwards across the Kirchenfeld Bridge

solstice winds unpick the days
strong enough to wrench hair & teeth
from this shallow skin

the roar of skinny trees
surely signals eradication—
a world & its sister blown flat

but the trees are up on their toes
getting as far as they can up into the wind
stretching with their eyes screwed up tight
making each leaf & twiglet as long as possible

rocking in exultation as the sun goes down
towards sleep lined with amber crystal

hope blown out of all proportion

the grater clogged with ginger

warm gusts from the funnels
dodge & turn on deck
ghosts of hope

a host of midnight lights
shows the ferry approaching
then passing by

a generation keeping to some flawed
& unacknowledged schedule

night sits out on deck
flappy wet wind pouncing on metal edges

the thick cream coats of paint
hug our gentle rust breathing its waves of pain
beneath the hopeless surfaces

fat ferry engines sound like the neighbours'
generator a few gardens away
powering the tools & components
of some unexceptional hobby

I lean over the rails
high in the saturated starless sky
& imagine Dante or someone saying
it's no good turning up the gas
if the pilot light's gone out

I gave you everything

storms continue to bat the country about

the cat has come home
after six months
savaged by hunting

I gave you nothing

I have the south in the pit of my stomach
in the gaps in my skull

I feel my places being taken
as dusk falls & swans fly in
from the west in loose skeins
veering left just above the water
to touch down into north-west wind

I need to be a thousand miles south

as for us
sometimes even galaxies which collide
being mainly space & silence
simply pass through each other
with just a few local clicks & flickers

this cheesy Italian meatball
my heart
is in my stomach

as I wash a diagram of my life blue
my stomach isn't in it

it's true what they say
with art you're up a tree
without a paddle

I was eleven
when I saw the trucks
head off towards the border
loaded with chunks of crystalline sphere

I flicked a plectrum in the collection plate

longing to bang my gong before the void
without some ventriloquist
interrupting the sexy echo

so it begins
opening like a last Sunday afternoon on the Shannon
the shaded & endless light acoustics of no return
(these shaded & endless light acoustics)

I eased the edges back
& stood in the desolation
of sufficient space

I hear shutters opening
sense warm olive oil
    garlic
   peperoncini
my liver lisping in a pan
see a brush dancing in a dark kitchen

before a vision of small lights
stepping down through the night
to a first glimpse of the Mediterranean

my inner streets awash in the bright
burn of Ligurian wine
above the first cool shock
of clear water under the keel

you cannot start without trusting the art

you clot
of nature you
language made incarnate

we stopped on the Via Appia
still ringing to the trundle of the train
heading south towards Rome

watercolours unpacked
we looked in vain for water
so we piddled in a dish
to resuscitate the earthly shades
the terracottas & ochres into pages of a new land

I've been moving
I've been moving into the imagined view

though one part of me
has always been silhouetted
against a northern moon
hands in pockets
ruefully signing a landscape of snow

there are dives you can't pull out of

breath-grey ones every hour
vertiginous Prussian blue ones   a few a decade

& the steep white swoop
                         OK
                         so
                         far
                         etc
     in the middle of all this
the trombone insists on an
interesting range of attention-seeking strategies
& we cannot but defer
if only we could remember what had been sacrificed
to be here   blah grumble mumble   rake your marbles

Barry Guy laces benign pins
between the strings of his lover's body
hunkers into the first thinly veneered scrum
a high ball in a falling sky
13 July 1995 sweating smoke in the Vortex
where Evan Parker changes a wheel
on soprano without pulling in from the fast lane

now there are two paintbrushes
quivering weft in the double-bass's dark loom
the pigment along the inside of my arm
is tingling in the tasty decay whose aroma
is music that bag of ants
Rory Gallagher dead
Formication Blues man

gulls swing below
your despair regular shallow breaths
like the strand at low tide
with Venus over the north Clare coast
or is that Vesuvius?   carved out
hollow doubt   a memory or a shadow
a harp soundbox toiling in longshore drift
my small buoyancy way out

today I walked in fields of stone
dense flora budding in crevices beneath the wind
fingering alkaline soils of their own making
among acid slabs of grey rock
      a picture of my mind
      a bit of the universe
      no trainspotters

I'm only after getting off the boat
I'm taking the sway to the top of the hill
to gaze down at the sea playing
                      Kenny Wheeler on 'Sea Horse'
listen to the music
give me a new sense of my nose in space
like swigging from a tin
inventing the weather forecast
watching the gods flap on the margins of vision
empty fertilizer bags   soft touches

~

the night stirring sea
an outline of Ischia
Naples again

a quiet harvest of lights

memory shadows

a gull's wing below

marriage   Munich   moths

let me list:
Cézanne   the greatest teacher in my eyes
Kandinsky   who said stop interfering with nature
                  & get fluent on the Kosmic Kolour Keyboard

Delaunay   Matisse   Goya

the business of parallel & interpenetrating universes
has more to do with painting
than with the new Gothic physics

it's a question of tone & specifics though:
shelling peas opening the seam something falls
then flutters up to perch on the ceiling
      Wagner's on the radio on tiptoe
      in his chef's hat his penis protruding
      through a gilded doughnut that hums when full
      the creepy splendour of its seasickness
      its relentless stress-mismanagement
      striding & salivating like a wobblyman

suddenly I want a drink that's crisp strong & see-through
well it's not always clear what's needed
bollocks
what's needed is justice and work

more interesting than this or that
is the headlong & eternal
moment of creation
there are certain ditches you can't jump
without throwing all your kit over first

now this painting is all about how
on the day of my death
I'll open a warm roll with my thumbs
squash goat's cheese in it
tip in a glistening artichoke heart
     straight from the little glass jar
insert four slim anchovy fillets
a flurry of rocket
& a finely cut caper

    I'll take my roll
    & a stein of red wine
   into this room starring

Ensor	Masks Confronting Death	1888
Rodchenko	Non-Objective Painting Black on Black	1918
me	Twittering Machine	1922
Beuys	Tree in a Croatian Swamp	1944
yes & his	Neutralized Capital	1980

& Jean the cleaner
in wooden sandals
making things shine

West Coast
for Tom

from Dunwich to Galway
a swoon of legislation
in search of the graves
of the Beach Boys

just as each equation
includes both pork & patience
so grace touches your step
irrespective of destination
angle of incidence
pitch or yaw

a Union Flag
on a bendy stick
will still signify a caravan
selling hot-dogs

Tenor Legacy
for Steph

on the road across the globe
away from days of whine & neuroses
Suffolk for comfort
stowed in the boot
two scotch eggs & a fairy costume
the Sunday morning sea experience
sucks its bones & the beach
turns over inside us
you never get out of earshot
whatever the distance
however finely distributed the grit

suck & pummel the beach in your sleep
never lose the fear
I said you never get out of earshot

Joe Pass Live in Every Hedge

It is 8:50 in Hills Road Post Office
& an inappropriate breakfast sandwich
makes me think of you.
It must be pleasant to be caked
in cucumber & mayonnaise
(notwithstanding your predilection
for butterscotch angel delight)
unless you're a tuna.
I woke up with your face
in my eye & a thought in my head
like a line by John James but no
it disappeared as mysteriously as it had not come.

Real Book

eating silent shellfish in the mist
to Steve Swallow & the government

Barry McSweeney signing *Pearl* for Lynn

I can't help thinking
you can't help looking
at paintings with your face

Oystercatcher

1
a load of gutted loft insulation
stirs on the front lawn

an airy cake of yellow web & dust

we & the strange house
breathe in slight differences
through late winter nights
that resound to little adaptations
& imagined trespasses

the space above has increased

the January morning is a shallow basket
left by the dustbin
weightless
full of snow & brilliant tracks

2
the chalk stratum glows
between thunder & carrstone

a low tide behind
the sea wind come to life

3
a chimney unblocked
after 20 years

voices return
from undressed walls

it dawns on us
the oceanic surge through
seconds of disrupted grammar
the sea wielding sun
to open windows

4
shifting whispers of sky in the hearth
taste of stale air in cupboards

relative absence of paranoia

5
sticks of rot & woodworm
feed the reopened hearth

ease this decayed air out of the house &
mouth into the local star gale

6
the winds walking
waves on the sea

through the carpet
right to the fire

on the horizon
a white citadel

7
February quarter light & dawn smell
Rustin's Pure Turpentine
150 mil of titanium white

the last smear of indigo
breadcrumbs & linseed oil

the ache of the familiar versus
the ache of the unknown

the day's first oystercatcher lands
facing east

8
mussel beds sunk under the storm
top of the world whipped headless black

noise as of boxes being shifted
way below or above

hair-dark wind

9
trudging back off the low-tide mussel beds
a muddy Tesco bag full of late sun
& two pints of living shells

the making tide & blue angels
go about their business as usual

you can walk here so far into the sea
that when you turn around
the land appears
like someone else's and your own idea

Starfish

ochre orange mauve
a small implied vortex
its chubby roughness
sags damp on wet sand
at the mid-tide
apparently lifeless
in westering sun

yet lifted into evening light
each tube foot starts
walking through the air

Landing

First July light covered our sea with birds.
More than ever before rode the morning,
moving with a rhythm from the distance—
the bay, the chalk & sandstone, the moon's ghost.

Where do you stop? You stand on the landing
glowing between the front & back windows,
breathing in quiet light & making tide.
Life finally fits, like wine in a glass.

& before the birds rise, & tide withdraws,
you realize the tide is always high,
the great wish of sea, reaching for the moon,
staying constant as the Earth turns through it.

from The Green Hill

with the sound of steps going
up & around
to cover the same ground

turn on again
a kitchen light
which suddenly illuminates
the whole of our past
  garden surrounded by darkness

~

ghostly traffic out in the bay
      some port lights   a starboard light

   a few sound signals advising of presence

Peg

under the massive & still frost free
scintillation of piercing stars

the dog sits in a mild October gale
under the energised band of the milky way

demented with night

unwilling to come back
into the caravan

Liederkreis

1
morning appears like a
disappointing Heine website
moving towards the window
away from leaden pillows
she walks beyond horizons
of echoey b-sides

after dark we stand on
exposed & disused inner runways
the cold night marries
arctic depths inside our chests

2
I duck in & out of rain
searching for a gap in time
it won't be long now
is where I live
I pay the rising costs with philosophy
today I pulled the chain
on one of the holy wells of the self
I let a key slip into the drain
through the shining water running in the gutter
I made for the heartening glow below street level
escaping from the fog of Prague
into the arbitrary place for food & drink
I have become

3
no sooner do I feel the urge to leave
via the wonderfully decaying woods
than you confront me in my mouth
& stars bristle in my veins

how does the blackthorn make those lines
I keep breathing in
measuring the bleak expanding heavens
these trees would hold my grief
on the damp tips of their dark branches
but I jealously swallow it down
packing it tight inside my bones

4
finger my heart again
can you feel the footsteps echo in its cell
that bastard builder death lives there
bodging up a post-retirement nook
the endless racket has kept me awake
for longer than I remember
I wish the idle sod would get on with it
let me turn into sleep once & for all

5
you picturesque crib of misery
you mausoleum of my ease
my great town it's time for me
to say the toughest of goodbyes
goodbye to each burnished junction
where still she passes by
goodbye to that shining site
where I first saw her
I wish I'd never met you,
beautiful queen of my heart
then it wouldn't have ended this way
with me so inside out & out to dry
I never hoped to touch your heart
I never even wished for love
I just wanted to live a quiet life
inside the same air that you breathe

but you drive me away
your lips mouth cruel words
madness swarms through my body
its eggs hatching out in the wrecked hutch of my heart
I plod on with my heavy sack of self
& this worn out staff
until I put my head down in the distance
the cold hole fitting perfectly for ever

from The Summer of Agios Dimitrios

Wednesday 12th September

only after take-off
do you see a range of places
where you could have walked the dog
if only you'd had one
& those oddly-shaped bodies of water
which are never there when you get back
our heads in the clouds
& in the inner distance
we heard goat bells on wild promontories
the sea almost too bright to see
feral sea-nymphs nudging the rudders
of sailors who scratch their heads
under sea-stained caps
lick a finger & stick it in the sky
shrug
then put in for a bottle of Mythos
& a cheese pie
on the plank outside
in the sunny dust
peaches
bleached French beans
& a row of slightly deflated
weeping purple figs
at the height of their powers

Friday 14th September

the mountain top clear
of cloud I can hear
the sea under star

shapes above the eucalyptus
cicada plucking at
distance some say
Cygnus some Northern
Cross either way almost
lost in a fertile haze of milky
way a mosquito followed a
bat through the night & out
the other side to morning
shadow of the jasmine on
a bowl as I rinse out
the mop some say it's all
written but I'd fold it
again & again
until it fits my smallest
pocket & walk
into the water

Saturday 15th September

sun swallows behind
the violet rim of land
between sea & sky
an unfamiliar breeze
pecks the table
questioning our intentions & spelling
this page is held down
by the clips they use
to anchor tablecloths
in tavernas along the coast
the paper is sun-bright orange
then grey
now lit by an electric glare & almost dead
if you don't know how to spell a word

you can always use another
the garden hose doesn't reach
the bottle brush tree
so we carry it six bowls of water
then back away
as it exhales

Sunday 16th September

the speechless water
Ritsos carried in his hands
reappeared in Elytis
near the church of St John
on whose day in midsummer
a child fetches water
from the local spring or well
& carries it back without speaking
every child in the village
places a small belonging
into the water
which is then covered
with a red cloth
the container is left
outdoors all night
so the stars may move over it
come morning
the cloth is removed
& each child's possession
is restored
now poems on
the future of the children
can be made

Monday 17th September

three people are poised
on the church tower
in Nomitsi
each at a different level
they allow
some sky into the structure
the next church
has a miniature door
& two long curving palm leaves
as tall as a person
framing the entrance
but the finest is
the last church
the metamorphosis
in which you hear
still the builders' voices
at different levels
the great clarity of the air means
you can shout really loud
many local calls can be made
without a phone
inside the church
a little light came in from here
& there the wooden offertory plate
was filled with change

Friday 21st September

it's easy now to get back
where we were
the place so hard
to reach at the beginning

just follow the road
& catch drops of rain
each fat as a fig
sleep involved much waking up
from dreams fuelled
by brown white wine & brandy
I couldn't save you from being pushed
into a woodland pond by a happy
animal part lassie part lion that
balanced its paws on your shoulders
until you toppled into waking
it's better to know the truth
sit on the step
& write in gentle rain

Sunday 23rd September

cover the cupboard in wet blue paint
reinflate the punctured dinghy
adding a see-through superglue
scab on its hole
embark on an initial voyage
but neglect to placate Poseidon
who hisses underneath as we paddle
along the sharp Ionian seaboard
it's practically a Seferis poem
until a plastic oar twangs in the air
& half the crew abandons ship
the water facilitated quick descending
light through clear green pulses
& waverings onto serrated limestone
craters cupping clutches of rounded stones
& thin fish with green & purple patterns
you couldn't tell from the surface how

you swam suddenly out over great
depths the water darkening like evening sky
& all forms become indistinct
hovering through evening light
at two in the afternoon
sun fierce on the blue
& unseen lines on my back

Monday 24th September

underground passages
unexpectedly complex
you can explore only so many
a lifetime isn't enough
as they say about Rome
Roma—non basta una vita
but some tunnels are dull
& there's the time you waste
prevaricating at junctions
the path you're on is your own
many of the passages
are low & narrow the water shallow
pebbles clear a foot below the surface
small lights illuminate the route
the boat rocks if we move
we duck our heads & proceed feeling
the roof recede beyond our reach
a breathtaking sensation
the world expands until a limestone spur
cuffs you on the shoulder as you snake
into the mountain the stone sky drips
slowly growing down to meet the ground
wherever it is rich enough
wherever it is rich enough
the ground rears up to meet it

Sunday 30th September

dawn at the end of September
the waning moon loosely moored
in the stirring eucalyptus tree
the constant unfolding of surf
muttering below the scent of jasmine
on which the night's last moths alight
brushing the flower which hardly moves
a touch like breath that's situated here
against the down on your forearm
& then is gone & it's lighter now
a little owl calls across chapel beach
as the light is turned off in the kitchen
four pine needles & their shadows on the rock
the dark nodding mid-morning sea
through the skin of the water
& deeper into another element
entering the ultramarine cave by touch
& in the still shadows of a sultry afternoon
honey slid glistening over figs

Tuesday 1st October

it's a new sun as long as we're moving
& it's rolled up over the mountain tops
by the process of standing on the ground
looking beyond the wall of the garden
there's something for everyone in the new
world supersite at a junction near you
not-for-profit provision of power
for light & heat & transport & communication
you can even have some water from the sky
without filling the pockets of shareholders

you can hear & say these words everywhere
TV radio oracle papers many heavens
the plates we left outside on the table
throughout the autumn nights are full of change

Tuesday 2nd October

it's a long way to the gates of Hades
you can get there via the Diros caves
please wear a hard hat
because the ancient people who lived here
stopped doing so
when an earthquake brought the roof down on their heads
& the roof was a mountain
this should have been the entrance to the underworld
& indeed it was
as is the place where each of us is standing
they used to rearrange their dead
into neat heaps until the big heap happened
& there was no-one left to rearrange them
until quite recently
thousands of mysterious points
shine down from the ceiling
there's always so much falling from the sky
her hands cupped in sleep

Monday 8th October

they tied up the Temple of Apollo
in a canvas bag to keep the rain off
now it can't see over the vale

to the sea past the charred leaves
of Arcadia for miles
conceptual art in pewter
copper & matt black
the dark edges of the road
feathered with soot
& printed shadows flicked the way
the roaring wind of fire went
limping & sprinting
some of those caught
on the tinder slopes died
some were elsewhere
& lost everything
but their scorched hunger
& a sifting ache
for continuity that still
whispers the landscape
hurts most where local people
through dignity pride or modesty
had already pared things down
in their old age
which was swept away
in one the century's brightest nights
black empty tins on the lintel

Tuesday 9th October

black rusty shutters
clap in the breeze
new green growth
can be seen on the ground
by all those still here to see it
in places the fire
exploded in waves

roaring in every direction at once
stark photographs of the dark heart of light
developed as far as the mind could see
in the distance the legend of the beast
the petrol-soaked rag tied to a back leg
with electrical cable & then lit
so the fire seeds were sown in a mad plunge
zig-zagging through the world in an orgy
of fricatives & plosives
echoing around the desolate
cave of the mouth

Thursday 11th October

start with a stunning marble threshold
monsters blades & vines proclaim
a heady blend of opulence & power
carved in crystalline detail around the door
beyond a less impressive space
where working people looked at the bare floor
while straight-backed proprietors stalked past
with modest movements of their mouths & hands
a model of courtesy & restraint
one in a million one in a million
dressed in silk that falls straight to the ground
with the fluid grace of a poured fine wine
then there's a dark backyard of blood-marked earth
where feral cats kill with economy

Monday 15th October

a car came by every evening
loudspeaker clamped to the roof
shouting about a politician
& how we'd go forwards together
forever starting with the forthcoming
but the car had already passed by
accelerating to the next village
I carry on cooking sausage pasta
with Greek bangers & a very curly
chilli pepper when the same car
comes racing back past the chapel as if
something important had been forgotten
this time the car's going slightly faster
& disappears without a word

Thursday 18th October

some weeks last months
you slipped off the red dress
in the twinkling of two eyes
we walked the deserted city
through the fragile summer night
with light purposeful steps
& no idea of where to go
a completion of autumn sunshine
settles through the gaps
of the garden behind the house
where if you close your eyes
you see trumpets & watercress
paintbrushes & brandy
a small stone dish of salt
skin under very thin clothing

& the mistakes
like cactus-flavoured ice-cream
refusing to melt in the gutter
but here's a butterfly
with shapely lemon wings
& at the tip of each
soft orange patches
clapping together noiselessly
over your flowers

Friday 19th October

to reach Milia by car
says the map
turn right at Stoupa
drive through Pirgos
past the goats on the left who are still in bed
& the cows on your right who are not there
the sun goes unexpectedly behind
a scrap of cloud no bigger than your hand
held at the end of your arm in the sky
fast approaching the Milia junction
here we should turn right but go straight on
to Kastania because we like it
stop at the first church
St John's where a padlock is padlocked to
a padlock from which an old bit
of wire snares a nail in the door
lift the wire & go in admiring the way
your mass alters the shape of the space inside
with its small choirs of interlocking curves
& the dusty grey light
that whispers down to touch you

Saturday 20th October

we go on haunting the places we love
coming in from yet another angle
walking up the track to skirt the village
surprising the mad cat in the bin
who scratches wailing
at the sloping sides of the hollow box
then zooms out splayed against
the air with the plastic that held a
4-pack of beer round one leg
& a lolly wrapper on its ear
that is not a healthy diet
overshoot the village so you see it
well disposed below with its cats & dogs
craning their necks & tails at the humans
clambering down past vegetable terraces
to Agios Petros & its tower
in here it is best not to walk backwards
from the paintings into the dangling lamp
which flickers & sips holy oil
because it may tip all over your shirt
& not wash out even with Greek Omo

Wednesday 24th October

wriggling through a gap in Kalamata
through to the startling Sparta road
driving higher & thinner & tighter through passes
a rare cold precipice drops you breathing
& closing the window on vertigo
& ash from burned out sheds & tavernas
the ghost of a weighing scale hangs above
a blackened table as we park in a cloud

the windscreen wipers smearing damp red dust
in seeping arcs to show a rectangle
of charcoal on the ground beside the road
a bent metal sign whispers Honey
in grey ghosts of Greek & English script
where impenetrable thorn cover grew
a hunter steps through black calligraphy

Sunday 28th October

a church high above the Ionian
as the first windless day for a week ends
in a wide stillness in which sounds emerge
lapping this ledge: a woman talking to
a neighbour hundreds of feet below
a gun dog chained to a rusting tractor
barks with a hoarse & mournful hoot
a lizard flicks through a crack in the locked church
three different sheep bells neither harmonise
nor clash but inhabit the darker sound
of the sea far below which almost gasps
almost continuously & so it should
carrying for miles & years through the scrub
of this old basket of litter & stars

Tuesday 30th October

I got the mosquito with an orange
then I ate the orange: justice is done
in airports the blues is turned to trifle
& because travel makes you really thick

why not buy four kilos of Toblerone
& a bottle of Scotch for eighty quid
the engines start up so do the babies
howling over the lights of Piraeus
then we & the babies are swept up to
twenty-six thousand feet over somewhere
too much like Switzerland for its own good
above the earth in the dark thoughts turn
to Norfolk winter saltmarsh & footpaths
meeting at the edge of Brancaster woods
where colonies of snails roost in the trees
mid-evening over a place like France &
from this height the world is decorated
by humanity with gold & silver
lights of habitation embroidered over
the rich dark cloak of earth with moonlight
flowing down our rivers past the churches
schools & hospital blocks to the lighthouse
poised by the shimmering acres of sea
I foolishly thought that writing this poem
would make me happier & it did

from The Pistol Tree Poems

3

edging the lawn with worn long-handled shears
just above sea level   it's hard to understand why maps don't tally
with what we're walking up & down on
or why what's in the papers doesn't chime with anyone we know
& why of two rhubarb plants
the first should unfurl & rise like a magic Arabian tent
all high red poles & voluminous masses of cool green shade
whispering spices   while the second is barely alive
should we dig it up & replace it with ginger & a few ears of wheat?
measuring the garden for new fencing
the figures change strangely depending
on which end I start from—
it's impossible to get your bearings   futile & indispensable to try
I wonder if Heine's last note ever got to Camille?
a perfect fix will give only an impossible point
to dance upon: a cocked hat at least gives a small
badly-prepared triangle to cultivate & live in
where a robin flits through a white poplar
& an arpeggio of goldfinches veers into the birches
as for courses to steer
what with all these uncertainties of tidal stream & weather
boat speed & appetite   cross track error
horizontal dilution of precision   still   steer we do
I'd even choose rope not for its qualities of strength
knot & give   but with reference to our shared cack-handedness:
polypropylene makes a poor enough rope
but at least it floats when you misjudge & drop it
down the crack between some country or other
& the side of your dilapidated boat—
& it'll still stop the goat going off-piste for a go at
the artichokes   herb garden   or other goat
tonight I'd rather navigate like the Polynesians once did
imagining position from the sway

& underlying tendency of the waves
while assembling lyric maps which trace the shapes
made by the clearest of these clear stars
                              the Plough upended on the Wash
                    Scorpius gradually wheeling past the back garden
using bits of driftwood   seaweed   flotsam   finger marks
reflecting on a change in the weather & unusual sea level
Schumann on the radio paints in some extra sand-banks
for the oystercatchers & seals   & Heine's Fly
I often put in yellow instead of blue
& recall Buy Ballot's Law:
the low pressure area should be on your left
if you stand with your back to the wind
the house martins fussed & keened & banked all evening
till the light slid off the edges of the sea & land
in the hours after dark you can feel them
     tucked up under the eaves of the house
                    you can feel them breathing
as the tide quietly rocks towards the moon they're watching

15

you might like to visit Shrimpton   in her Marazion gaf
a tasty *crab & saffron tart*   then   *brill with broad beans & pancetta*
choc-ice in treacle   according to the Sunday Sport
            I'm burning you a classic   to stow onboard your head
        my sweet tooth says I wanna
        but my wisdom tooth says no
                        seems half a lifetime since I painted Eve
stumbling through allotment gates   her fig wrapped in a soft yellow pad
    of withered rhubarb leaves   *Bending New Corners* seemed to whisper
        through her p-pod   in my sketches she too was hopelessly drawn
I scumbled powdered milk & soot   into the greys her eyes required
            this is neither the time nor the place to claim English poetry
        has been insufficiently influenced by Lester Bowie's *Serious Fun*
        I remember when I first saw those fascinating maps
of library LP surfaces   deft edgy pencil flicks of recent trips
hiccoughs   scrapes   pissed lunges towards heaven
knows what or whom   a deep trench through *Rigoletto*
    as he wandered home in darkness   sarcasm & sweat drying somewhere
            untouched between the inside of his mind & the empty night sky
    Cecilia felt you couldn't have your cock & eat it   *in a consort of voices*
        had a jagged rip which sent the needle swerving inwards fast
        a one-legged skater from Marston on acid
            speeding straight for the only hole in the ice
            the whole question of taste fucked me up for years
                as I lisped & ached through lips   bronze-wound strings
                & dented tubing   some of the poems are sermons
                some stroke purring pussies with bells on in the sun
                                but all of them are songs
                                just as all of Bach is dance
                                but won't be in the morning
                    did I ever tell you about Cecily?
            autumn was brimming with mussels-in-cider
we had radiant lapfuls in warm terracotta   reflecting stars
    & a watchful blonde from Finistère   she photographed migrating birds
            had to catch the midnight train

                        the paper glued inside the box lid
                    showed sparse hieroglyphs & arcane strokes
                        on an otherwise white ground
                         drawings of sin on the soul
                          birds assembling to leave
                                    an improvised notation of
improvisation
I sometimes see Maderno's statue in the night   her obsession with virginity
was partly her distaste for knackers & crannies
partly the spectre of the Madonna
but mainly wanting to wake up dead
turned & tuned into nothing but art

25

Mare che fiumi accoglie

Veronika was hopelessly drawn to Tom's smothered chops
you're the only one here not chasing tail   she crooned
        (which wasn't   strictly speaking   true)
        as she eased herself out of her mermaid costume
making me spoil the track by overdubbing 2 & 3 on 1
        l'angelo nero persuaded Schwanda the Bagpiper
to pork around with trollops   smoke in public places
tinker with strangers' appendages & duff designer trinkets –
even blow down the end of drugged octopuses
    reworking maritime ballads   & blues-inflected shanties
    into glistening yards of slightly twisted spawn
        his soul was as stuffed with sin's fat roe
        as an infected gap in the head with bright lime mucous
        full of the salty tang of young sea-lettuce in spring
one day   poised to abuse a beached whale   at Brancaster
Schwanda was saved   by a mystical German sea creature called
the Omniscient Mussel   sung tonight by Jill Grove (mezzo)
   Schwanda der Dudelsackpfeifer
   let me tell you   pronounced the Mussel   in gritty German
   you are coming to a sticky end   as usual
   having a whale   of a time
   but dribbling your prodigious gifts into the sand
   you're giving skateboarding a bad name too
fuck off   said Schwanda breathlessly   lighting up a Camel
you're not even in this opera   *it's just poetry in motion*
    yet Schwanda was given another chance
      & returned from hell without that natural backward glance
        I myself have just been practising   modal shifts
         & have tipped the spit   out of a student model
          (soprano)   it's the end of an era
            this could be the last time   I don't know
Helen didn't even go to Troy
she spent that decade in Egyptian resorts

doing yoga & aerobics
Tai Chi   organic gardening
the odd poetry workshop
auditioning for girl bands
& snuggling up with Menelaus for counselling sessions
today we're doing the history of the mind
a bit of distance learning   Kurt Vonnegut said
we're here on earth to fart around

31

Attended by two fallen angels and an evolving mollusc

in the absence of a nozzle for the old green garden hose
I once again succumb to wrinkled pink thumb cramp
fanning ghostly rainbows at the beans & rhubarb
turning through glistening arcs of soft wet light
towards the disused lighthouse & the west
                swooping swags of mist
slowly settle on the seedlings
& the midweek nymphs depart:
diverse birds emerge with expressions like mad pirates
seeking beakable earth after the dry spell
we regard each other sideways
as the sky turns farfetched Catholic mauve
filled with aching Bruckner endlessness
the spacious clarifying dusk sung by the first few evening stars
daily vastation   after tea   a dry fly cast into the silence
where any weight there is is in the line
              it's been a funny month
I swapped that tarnished tenor sax
for a scuffed black ocean-going canoe
& we found out how much is closed
with the help of new maps including OS Explorer 250
constructed on Transverse Mercato Projection
Airy Spheroid   OSGB   (1936) Datum
                a deer & her fawn at TF670283
so we stood motionless   gently watching each other
breathing like in a nature poem
but not the one I wrote yesterday:
alpen/alpen/digraph cluster/I felt sadder/after lunch
maybe I'll change it today as we had bacon
        the Omniscient Mussel is relaxin'
    in a creased slate-coloured shell suit:
  wassup purrs the benign bivalve
hi OM   I say   why have they barricaded Gipsy Green? [TF691424]

   the local suits heard the goat-girl was coming replied the mollusc
the lost & visionary goat-girl
with her unsponsored songs of tomorrow
                        at the end of our walk
we saw the road from the other side

45

so tomorrow it's off to King's Lynn
1   fit tow-bar
2   have Great Aunt Maisy spayed
3   investigate suede wall art
       on speedway themes
we like to stop off on the way
admire the queen's trees
& the bristling fields
where teams of East Europeans
fill vast trailers with tiny things
for other folk to eat
      sometimes it's hard to straighten up
George said
      stella maris
      stella maris
not a good name for a car
a fire-eater at the East of England show
or the last human cannonball in Yorkshire
      it's such a wide & enchanted evening
the almost empty beach
touched with the last thin voices
from an endless wealth of languages
addressed to different
dogs & gods
partners & children
a long way away
& now the night tide
covers everywhere
we've been standing
but tomorrow is another day
until we get there

early autumn morning thought
    you heard your footsteps
        coming back to meet you
            the faulty street light clicks
          buzzes   & hums a new tune
  in front of   the Hôtel de L'Avenir
the duck standing just out of sight in the fog
where an empty sports shop still promises
new away kit now available
            it's the kind of day
        when new people are conceived
      by the universe   are born
    or die forever   twist the knife
  in distant strangers   or enrol on courses
      called things like Yoga for Begonias
      for a moment it looked as though
        the world could be unpacked
          from all our damaged cases
& cleared from all these shredded papers
            dishonoured contracts
              stained canticles
  & left out all night to shine among us
        luminous mist suspending
a tree's last wet apple
              while somewhere electrical
    Sonny Rollins
                      live in Toulouse
      plays
          More than You Know

51

Nick Cave is in the house

   & as the Omniscient Mussel mused
  on Len's pink tights & bristles
it recalled blobs of molten lead
  dropped from a height of one thumb
    into tumblers of very cold water
      making shapes & signs
          such as this front end of a prawn
     some kid outside with issues
    in the glowing Tuscan gloaming
   shouts   *tonsils are bollocks*
 for her own reasons   seven coals fuse
in a draft from the forest out the back   cadmium
  orange thoughts   sent fluttering through
   the diminishing fuel of autumn fires
   the bronze long gone for cannon in Ferrara
              it's not too late to start again
red dust sifts down through pin-pricks in the master
  buffering now 49% complete
   sea-food inspiration &
     Aretino's *I xvi modi*
he cut through the old man's skin
     to find the empty nest
    that death had made there
ah the Light   the Pisan
Chips   the Beer
the Lightly Battered Haddock
these are just a few of the dance steps
performed tonight on moonlit Gypsy Green

53

'There is nobody here but us chickens'

    when Haydn
     went to Slough
      to see the stars
    he tinkered with creation
     & explored certain
   new yoga positions
        like
  Feed Wrong End of Dog
   Wash Foot in Caravan Sink
    & Kick-start the Transit
but in the western ghats
  we watch cloud goats
 & listen to the notes
  almost turning
      into solid air
   we steel
    ourselves
  but not for long
  sleep-spindles point
   towards a club
where you can go
  to be yourself
   or sit & knit
some little coats for chickens
    the bones & mortar
 will turn to beige paste
   & thick bars rust

Minchia, che bella!

Lynn's made ginger & rhubarb muffins
   as gifts for the Spring Oracle   spongy
sumps of treacle rising up towards a new moon—
        the oracle (which actually prefers
Norfolk Pork & Haddock Chowder—a tradition
    accidently launched last year)   ordains:
       throw away your watch strap
          place watch on tongue
       & shut your mouth
     fortunately
we have kept a few for midnight feasts
 & share one with the O.M.
 esconced in a birch-twig cabin
the size of a fist or heart up in the Magic Willow
[see Quintet on St. Cecilia's Day for more details]
    the O.M.—now snug in a muffin—mutters
  let the moon grow out of your head to fill the sky
& change the sound of the wind with permanent readiness
  for seconds as the earth turns in its sleep
    & a city drops to its knees in the dust
       a few fleas settle back down on the stray dog
         by a fountain in the dark piazza
 the sun will burn out your eyes
    unless you project its power onto paper

63

(1ˢᵗ version/ take 4)

    the Omniscient Mussel is listening:
hark   Reincarnation of a Love Bird
 & recall how Mingus
     could click gummy limpets into the sea
               with a miniscule flick of his fingers
    Lynn & I finish Tippexing the plimsolls
   ready for the opera   at the Fakenham Gas Museum
it's a familiar plot: beauty is stolen by the regime
  then used as a model for culture & the Madonna
       who oversees & overrides each
              twitch & simmer of temptation
       from a glowing niche set high up in a wall
              dividing this world from the next
       a virtual planet refreshing the decrepit
      again that aria   *hose down my tail plumes*
in a white-tiled room   *& bake me into Narnia*
had many sighing into their vanilla tubs
Eric Dolphy buzzes the current on bass clarinet
Paul Bley colouring gaps in the air soft & loud
    Mingus restringing the actual pylon
        with live cable & plucking a lament
for every bird no longer on the wing or wire

65

zuppa di cozze alle tarentina

        the Omniscient Mussel
        was rinsing its hinge
        in a thimbleful
        of Pedigree
        & listening
to a Jackson Brown tribute act
            called Snow Patrol
an oar enters the water noiselessly
  disentangles a knobbly stir of weed
     pushes a wobbling dimple
back into nodding & dazzling plain
      every mind-map becomes
     sandcastles after two days
     & nights out in the rain
        I resume
      my distance learning
      course on absence
        management
     by evening a thin
    skin forms on each
      idea & shivers

67

that's one of the places yetbutaswell

it was Beethoven who first observed
the road to Rotterdam was paved with chub
well it's not cramp & it's not flamenco
I just lay my burden down
& someone picked it up
& ran out of the station
you damn right I got the blues
though the bushes now lean in
with more than a Hint of Mint
& the Vauxhall Astra Green
which haunts the season's magazines
    it is true that in our younger days
we were meteorites over Burnley
but now anonymous visitors
have to rattle a poker around in our mouths
when it is time to start the day
so many August stars have plummeted
from the windy darkness between
Perseus & Cassiopeia
since I first took Leonora for the coalman

69

It's a bit like when you point at something
that you want your dog to notice, and the dog
just looks at your finger.

  here in the U.K. they're knitting poems
                      to celebrate the centenary
                                of the Poetry Society
  & shrews make little partings in the grass
before owls pounce then plummet upwards
  to perch in the branches of dead elms
      among forgotten constellations
I remember when we met in west Vienna
      I had skate
  you had the dark Russian sole
we talked about the inabilities of silence
  to express immensity or domicile
the separate subclumps of the Virgo Cluster
the need to scratch at the skin
  of some tambourine till blood peeps out
the motto of the mollusc: what is
  human about humans may be *logos*
    but life remains the slow construction of a home
      in unspeakable tide & hunger

71

Perhaps I eat to persuade myself that I am somebody

a long procession ambles past the window
to mark the golden age of Norfolk art
which begins each evening
at about this time
out in the autumn night of deft
inequity & stars the sky cradle echoes
to many grey & white appliances
another Mannheim Rocket
& reruns of Popeye Doll
wedged between the shipping forecast & dim news
eggs on the boil rock knocking in a dented saucepan
through a mysterious smell of Swarfega & lime-pickle
o season of radio halos
  it's as if Heine were just around the headland
trolling for zander & listening to
some local country music
from the days of Tory happiness
when donkeys wore high hats

73

una sera cosí strana e profonda
che lo dice anche la radio

          it's well after midnight
        as the final trucks
       heave the last of the Fair
      from cliff-top mud
     to the sound of Lucio Dalla
    bonfire roots pulsing in a S.E. wind
   oystercatchers stare from outside
a hovering disc of orange light
  & then it's the dog zig-zagging
   down the garden
    too busy & early
     for a busy early morning piss
      that finds it
       in the vegetable patch
        mucky & malnourished
         with clingfilm wrapped around
           the raw stumps of its wings

75

what to you now are eyes
in nights to come will be stars

                now the pickled onions are fantastic
        a first bite twists the spine 20 degrees
        anti-clockwise with left shoulder dipping
        so folks developed language & language
        developed people which helped us knock through
        but also dumped too much weight in the boot
        thus fucking up most front-wheel drives & those
        who squat in the backs of caves wondering
            what star-light might be like in ideal worlds
            instead of smacking fat pigs with ping-pong
            bats from which the rubber mat flaps free or
                licking Swindon nymphs in the fairy-light
                    lit gloom of St Cecilia's Day where
                Purcell no it's Mahler is humming you
    mustn't enclose the night inside you you
you must flood it in eternal light

77

I'd like to do a little more wrong
at this point.

        winds aspirate with ice
     from hearts of darkness
west of Ely
   twitch the old moleskin slacks
      as night follows day
         & decades of fen—
                 over a flask
       of magic-mushroom soup
          the O.M. admits that this
            is as good a time as any
      for me to realise my ambition
       to drop-kick a warmed-up
   chicken & mushroom pukka pie
             with my bare foot
for the purposes of divination

79

God does not play snooker

the Omniscient Mussel is fresh in
from a gruelling tour of my pizza
& is sporting a perky Boy George hat
that may soon be catching on in Norfolk
in the middle of the seafood spiral
there is a path down to a cavity
in which a liquid xenon target waits
for more detailed news of the universe
even in the shadows of cheese & caves
there is oppression of a talc-tipped kind
echoes of dead voices coming in waves
to smother & silt up the expectant mind
even in a night of cold rain I sense
something more than water in the water

83

ideas about diseases of ideas
drift home from the paradigm shift
hide slivers of a broken bell
between the boat's timbers
with apps to propitiate the jumbies
rowing towards the edges
out over the site of floating markets
past the sunken cages where we learned
to click our fingers underwater
a gibbon climbs the last stilt
of a rotting pontoon to show us all
the length of a fish it once nearly caught

87

north Lynn Duende

I have dusted the stuffed weasel
& placed it in a sunlit niche
tinged submarine by stained glass
made with patience & the urine
of prepubescent redheads
in centuries & minutes gone by
even the O.M. is sleeping
rocked in whispering sea-green dreams
spasm of tangible absence
rose & broken into cold song

89

antiphonal
Ambrosian
it will soon be time to end the preparations
O Spanish bluebell girls of Galway Bay
O little tin of Tanglefoot think 25
cashier confirmed over 18
wtrcrss spinach rckt
a stately procession passes the back of my mind
change

91

even before the goddess
of love & her
horny henchpersons
eased the bamboo sliver
through the tough kebab chunk
of my heart
I glimpsed others sneaking
to the woods for fuel

93

David Chaloner Collected Poems
didn't he & flew some in my life
o little grebe slide sideways by
on what appears to be the surface of a river
my bird is my wand
I think I'll say that to the memory
of David who is in the zone

99

the OM snaps my tooth-pick & buries it
certain fadoms under Old Hunstanton beach
the goat-girl & diverse demi-muppets
are gathering to do the dance   farewell

101

it is time to suck the tender sticks of Stockbridge Arrow
dipped in tangy latin sherbert
& redraft my translation of Handel's Green Prats

105

just time to pull on the feathered leggings

from Lynn Deeps

1

I see you board a west-bound bus in clothes
that nearly didn't make it & will not
tire of rubbing you up the right way
just as the seasons look out the window
in the first draft there will probably be
some gravity-related images
but it's best to break through those straight into
heaven sent these moist musical landings
it's a mumbling coalition after
my own heart not to mention the spumy
bowsprit of my voyage round your headland
it looks like we were caught in each other's
headlights & glove boxes for the finest
sentence in the history of transport

4

as further uncontrollable urges
whistle the north in sideways down the wash
to lift the top right off our potting shed
my mind returns to times that never were
like you in one of those swerving surges
in a day-glo & pneumatic lifeboat
your hand clutching the important hard bit
we used to grill collateral for lunch
steadfast in our hatred of butterflies
& their selfish brassica ravishes
the siren always took us by surprise
& is blu-tacked to the back of my mind
whose singed walls still echo with the first time
I ever explored your fishing village

5

of course some said at this stage of the game
is it wise to dive through the boundary
just buy some head-socks & take a picnic
along to a Joanna Newson gig
we cut the grass & think she may have done
I've got a brand new pair of rollerskates
& I left my heart in Newport Pagnell
but in the end we chose to escape through
a tunnel & thence by microlite to
sparsely populated regions such as
the old days eventually grew out of
we consulted the Fakenham birdbath
bulging ice lens still ignoring twilight
yet galvanising our faces in moon

8

this may have been you smiling in the dark
& that may have been your left stocking top
the asymmetry of the saxophone
I don't think you can call that a salad
although up to your elbows in growbag
you & the fire whisper sensible routes
through a complete history of power cuts
you even got me up on the dance floor
along with the tips of your fingers & things
in umber pubs smelling of cigarettes
& the small faces turned up in the night
to the gentle Wicklow rain for instance
through the fragility of eastern night
you make the light last longer on the water

9

daddy was a rafter in a coal mine
mummy deconstructed cardboard boxes
out behind the Co-op on weekday nights
with some help from the other immigrants
it was tricky to focus on weeding
the kitchen with you in your nomad shorts
& modified onion-chopping snorkel
yet still we made our way through the cliches
of sentence construction & assumption
by planting conkers in window boxes
then trundling down the aisle at 3 a.m.
towards the waiting pilchards & shampoo
yes love was always in the air but that
wasn't usually where we wanted it

10

though it's true that we won't last for ever
tonight we ought to put the dustbin out
things have a habit of lasting longer
than the daily mail says they're going to
I woke up this morning & it was still
the night before I tried to go to bed
a grope of hunger drifts in on the breeze
from the chip-shop which closed six hours ago
you don't need a tardis to fuck with time
it's best to jig along its back with love
until the caravan tips right over
that's why we don't plug it in to the grid
we just set light to stuff in handy fields
usually starting with each other

Poly-Olbion
for Roy Fisher

& this pub goes back to the last ice age
when Brutus ambled into Buckfastleigh
clanked sacks of silverware onto the bar
& ordered brioches & cappuccini

my great-grandfather was Aeneas
he boomed   to the bright strains of a French march
soon Spanish brandy seethed between us
Al Pacino glowing around the bay

so many separate blue receptors
debating permissable harmonics
& whether English is fit for singing
but at Christmas it remains the custom

to soak a goose's neck in lard & whisky
before sliding it into a mason

from Behoven

1

we suddenly lost interest
in such impossible pasts
lifting our heads towards
the river elsewhere
a new jetty stood beside
the old beyond repair
time mends an idea
slips its moorings
swings out into the current
& a kneeling figure
works on
pausing only to reach
for three more nails
& place them gently
between her lips

2

hello
cuckoo   drunk   I
come through hedges
sideways in September twigs
flick back & whip you
in a list of
reasons to be cheerful
with asterisks

3

      screw up page & wipe stars
     appear & tighten
     screws on loft-ladder
      tip-toe between Bo
       Diddley & a Renoir lavender
        ribbons in a mass of red
            hair run for the bus
       bed pushed to the window
      head sticking out into the sky
          a cantilevered plank
        relieves neck muscles
vans brought morning in the rain
however many nights the head
stayed out the rent remained
 the same fuel bills rose & turned red
         skip to the loo
         & sing a ring
          of shaving cream
              & rust   no credit

6

        the song's high fitful
        clarity surfs churning
        low-pressure systems
         relentless on-shore winds
          & a new moon calling
           water home to nowhere
                      seething tidal races
unnavigable gestures under glass
              & as the ink dries it fades
       like a note   as in note
            in the canopy live birds
   who've never seen the ground
    or heard of darkness falling
      fathoms below through
          cracked notions
trunks & hourly precipice
sooty mould dusts knuckles
in the ministry of growth
on the path behind the wood
a dusty nut
    splits & roots
       in the grey
             swaying rucksack

7

   rain on tiny wooden
   wheelbarrows & tramp steamers
   rabbits wash their ears behind
    the hill where we make it up
     these pretty trills transport
       soil beyond the national
           borders   the rabbit is dropsy
              flicks back into the guts
                  of the earth
          some died or moved away
            after summer fetes
             when strangers
        with sledge-hammers
         & shorts passed
        the whole piano
     through a bangle

8

        tomorrow fell from the sky
        with bits of food in the corners
           lenses rinsed in leaking
            vats of rough red wine
        any behaviour was being
    philosophical was my impression
of a bird being attacked by another
bird before they both sat quietly
            in a tree
  becoming beautiful is often
  the rhythm of concern
  rocking to & fro
before the knock on the door
with time & a mouthful of nails
  research shows
    the fate of each remnant
      to be more interesting
         than the fate of the bulk
         of each roll

9

                      bring bonny back
                        to the dockside
                           freed by waiting
                      for a morning
                of details
            tight trainers
       coffee containing pale grit
     a three-legged dog loping
    past grinning into the wind
      & the Copenhagen boat
           tending left
                  but several hands
           push it north-east
          to more frosty stacks
           of Baltic timber
  & potential passengers
 with indecision & fists
    stuffed in mufflers
             there is comfort in the story
                    sung without words
               a sunlit liquid shiver
           again we turned & tried
        remembering things
we'd never known

11

        impossible to creep up
       on the shelf from behind
       take your time eastwards
         in stomach-churning calm

       it's no good walking past like that
         even if it is called a patio

         lethargic topiary
        up beyond the mitten
         the face in space
        all chapped lips
          autumn stars

12

      apricots & black
    coffee by the mattress
     on the floorboards we breathed
      an aftershock of happiness

        cotton refuge

     glide between wing-beats

your memories coming up the stairs

        O Vienna!

13

    nocturnal reconnaissance

bring your own weather

    shacks of the deep south
    stacked with empty casks
    & the last seven words
    from the crossroads

the flag factory has closed
& crowds move down
  towards the docks
    waving wooden spoons

14

    a high-tide line
      of dead ladybirds
        in a world without sound

    pulse in a crevice

& words sail
into altered time of dark
red wine for several
  hours now years & geese
  migrating over
    the house

15

    an element of shanty
    far inland
    is irresistible
        now whistled
            now hummed
            we are night
    locked inside factories
        that pickle fish
            in Bonn

16

    he would stalk
        the winter quarters
            of the circus
        glaring at bears

17

        grave & shimmering
        restlessness this wasn't
        what they meant by
            salami keeping
        out the cold
intensities of autumn light
illuminate years
of reckless calm

       the ballroom now a surgery
          like a prayer in the night
            the poetry soars way up
towards the very edges
of the imagination
     almost reaching
          the hair-line

18

      sound check feel your way in
    before the hall fills up
      saw a house martin click by
          saw an inch from the back leg
              of the piano for the entry
        of the milliner's cousin Allegra
          feather bobbing to the loo
     in black   deft as in canary
    divertimento   road works

over the hill with a sapling
protruding from the top of the knapsack

     the fact that the song's
         without words
   allows one to continue

    clock tock   glass inflamed
  thin bell pings & sears
    the mind's four
         fissured towers

19

      miserable simplicities
  recline under the fingers
     whispering September
        plane leaves along the banks
           of the Seine cannot be heard
              from here unlike the fight
                    across the street
                  & the piano lesson
          that neither teacher
nor student attend

21

    they joined hands
        to form a lake
  in which nothing could live

    strands & coagulations
of night snagged
inside the sinuses
   lungs & vaults as
        the years pass

      oranges
blue with fame

26

    transformations of farewell
    revolved & swallowed
      I would keep you near by
          breathing
              pace the restless second
        question far
                into the night
    insomnia in C minor
    rawness through the throat
    eyes & pronouns
            freedom with bells on
                growing into
             nights full of lights
            that dance along
            imaginary alleys
          opening onto
        renovated streets

27

    I think therefore I hover
     hot & cold earth
      live & neutral turning into
        new dreams of Bach
          membrane
              ruptured
unity & resolution changed
          nothing about this
just another person in the world
            drinking coffee
      I think of happiness
            sleeping

on the banks
of inner streams
all our voices making up
for lost time
with lost time

28

sung across the loch
forever lost in Europe
remembering the cello
forgotten in a foreign
landlord's loft
some melodies are endless
the edges disappearing
in a mist that gently rises
over insight & perspective
trousers ready for the wash
determination to march on
senseless by learning the key
routes & striding blind
to the dimly-lit waterside bar
& a short-cut home underwater
nobody there
in the changing spaces between
moonlight shadows your own
tentative steps towards
the tether's end
a compartment
larger than the whole night sky
where this one love once lived
& yodelled across the cold
car-park in bare feet

31

        an uplift of daylit
         singing suspends
      the temporary sky
   in gaps between these folk
songs of the dispossessed
we watched when bread
was cast upon the waters
    & eaten by ducks
     the winter afternoon
      smells again of
       homelessness
     thus small waves fall
      along the edges
    deep seas of weariness
   pale flame burns unseen
in pale afternoons of sunlight
a bell tolls at low tide
  with unexpected modulations
    of tomorrow   not so much
     her words as her tone
    & a feeling that the sky
     awakes from hibernation
    while water surreptitiously
    frees the hull from soft
     sands of sense
         & knowledge

32

    sense of pit-props giving
      way below the head   galleries
        collapse & open into
         smoking moonlit gullies
        earthquake flutters
     paddle in dark water

       here where words
         were stars
          loom

Sabi

1

we started by creating
these soft holes in the air

2

when our chutes failed to open
we fell through a smell
of chocolate over York

3

this has always been the case

4

in the next parish
the second position
was called
the Egdon Nog

5

the sword discarded
is completed
by the slow
diplomacy of rust

6

in spring or autumn
stand or sit in awe
bit pissed

7

upon the creaky
bench of moonlight
transformation

8

two or three fingers
of spawn
in a plastic goblet

9

there are those
who say decay

10

there are those
who answer
preparation

11

o waxwing in the tree outside the Co-op

from Collected Letters

        I will not shout in God's bordello
    come rub your back on the bark of the pine
& dream a little dream of me
        we seem to be back on Line A to shake rattle
            & roar through the slightly hairy darkness
                we used to dream of tickling fish
              which would become our therapists
                  memories now of melting
                  come sliding off the roof
              the internet is down my love
                    the dog has lumps
    it's as well the days are getting longer
                Prêtresses de Bacchus
      sustain my delirium

an unexpected distance in the line
thrums from the lure
kinks & glimmers
silver frisking the picture
froth with whitebait
jerk a sea-bass
& from an open
upstairs window
the song again yearns
to enter a Tuscan
rearrange the word order
then change the words
into a kind of lay-by song
that will one day
be known as
dolce stil nuovo
 long after
  these three midges
   try to rub something out
     on the sky
       & infiltrate
          authorial presence

pumping the treadle　　unlike
on the sonic lathe　　　　many
of heaven powered　　electronic
by this tied-back　　　　　instruments
sapling tight as　　　　　　the Sound
the bow of a goddess　Lathe
noise & wood chip　　　produces
glitches beat & saw　　a unique
dust from trees　　　　　　wooden
to logs to legs　　　　　　　object
supporting such　　　　　at the end
exhaustion & a　　　　　　of each
muio interface　　　　　　　　performance

pace the sanded boards
of freshly emptied rooms

down there
the square

where we
accidently
danced
the *verdiales*
with a wasp

       mute

       just pedal
       or the monkey dies

                    ostinato (herbert 1866)
             articulation of the continuum blues
                        austin swallow
          unmeasured variation in the dawn song blues
                       austin goodwood
            trill syntax degradation in the bush blues
                         austin mini
             last light on roads through snow blues
                        austin gipsy
            banned underground songs of the 40s blues
                       austin maestro
            blue suede shoes across the border blues
                       austin princess
                 I believe I'll dust my broom

    &
   blu
  e fug
 ative a
 church
full of ang
ry bees when
some one brok
e a window first
vail rabbit cap then
patch together others
to make the sail I thought

     the water-table rose
   a bright stream reappearing
   along the length & breadth
    of the goat-track
     walking through changing
     twitches of perception
    a trumpet bounces off each
   each kitchen wall
the day's first empty tram
lit up at S. Giovanni
light around the edges
 closer for another second
  glance to quick gold flick
 this finch & zest of spring

from Site Guide

for Heine, and the Caravan Club

site 3

      the moon's   inexplicably abandoned
     in a different night of strangers
        devoid of pewter or cinnamon tunes
        or those of hawthorn   straw   or fennel
      larkspur / curlew
      she said when I end this line
   I'll count to three & you'll awake
forget this ever happened   1   2
            you can smell tcp
   for up to three weeks after you die
we opted for an hour or two of music
           luigi tenco megamix
             a bit of dr loco
      a transfer deal involving
        several pet shop boys
   with a neighbour's plastic suitcase
     she left in the rain before dawn
    in her I fucked leonard cohen t-shirt
      the wrong registration number
        etched on the caravan window
          there is nothing in the field
          except this empty grapefruit half
                two slugs nestling in the
                brilliantly white soft bottom

site 6

                    it only takes a moment
              to find a space
              disconnect
                  stare out of the window
                        welcome home
                  get used to living
    without a coherent world view
        in a temporary house
        called *wet paint*
a building made entirely out of doors
  allotment architecture is
the region's source of civic pride
 deconstructed palettes
  irregular lengths of unplaned timber
    openings hinged with strips of bald tyre
      swallow the sun with the sea
          as you swim through
        the edges of the world
          it moves up & down
              three millimetres
      on your neck   & tickles
     your body turning blue
        before being
mounted on wheels again

Site 11

    put the sparkle back into your privacy cubicle
    with a durable sojourn in one of the south's
      most northerly excuses & compliments
            twang your awning peg
        nestled where the sun rarely sets
         or indeed rises you will savour
    factory shopping outlets you'd forgotten
       & get back in touch with your own dutch quarter
           where traffic noise can be expected
            enjoy the local cycle-path or goat
       before numbing your remaining senses
            with a tasty german import
      & glimpses of the region's frozen laundry
       sculptures in the awesome precincts
           of where to choose a sofa
         the legendary dwarfs' causeway
          & the angel of the north
        are just a short flight from
the end of your optimistic suspension
of disbelief as a twenty-pound deposit
is required for the electronic barrier
  guided vegetable preparation may be
    available depending on season & staff
      disciplinary procedure outcomes

from 18

1
fairest
it is time
to fly like an eagle
you might
want to take
your boots off first

2
again we bit
into the insides
of our own mouths
remoulding the horizon
squeak
home on the range

3
run tongue over
scar tissue
another year has passed
in which no one
has employed
the inflatable canoe

4
the last place
to look
for mosquitoes
is in the dark
& inaccessible hollows
of your own flute

5
& this is where
the new nationalists
shaved her head
& left four tufts
in place of children

9
Dave Shrimp says
the big society
will be surrounded
by fires of bald tyres
& borders of yew

15
they are eating
boots of softest leather
when you mow mushrooms
they say in deep
serious voices
woffle

18
you will take tiny walks
in a tiny garden
damsons & mint
the stars of autumn slowly reappear

from Interscriptions
(with John Hall)

1
a skin is forming in the medium
riding incarnation through marine hues
& resonant halls of two-way mirrors
the script smooth & tight as scar tissue

3
the imprint suggests ambiguous tracks
scratched hieroglyphs of the sky & current
it may be an inviting tunnel
but it's also the way to the surface

5
they were trained to shoot up the standard post
& grow straight along regulation wire
these colours may put on weight as they dry
it's best to keep moving in case you set

7
start with a scar or leaf or syllable
then imagine somewhere for it to live
begin anywhere but the initial
voiceless dental non-sibilant fricative

9
leper hospital transformed into a
regally-appointed private chapel
the next glowing monument to piety
ravished with harmonies of air & grace

11
stuff the odds & starts in scuffed blue hold-alls
they change the speed of the whole carousel
I am available for work & food
spot someone moving in one of the bags

13
what if the words were to leave you
beached on interior sandbanks until death
dumb whiteness dissolving harmonic blues
the rind & husks of hope unmoved by breath

15
she said not all the stars are charted
city constellations from one flight
to another seethed & parted
the music changed the way we breathed for years

17
sibilance & seaweed in the shadows
beneath the lip of a tilted cup
the words of many drown inside us
turning into our disfigured dreams

19
the luxury of resonant spaces
is still song lodged in the throats of others
candles flickered script to stretching figures
lasting longer than any one thought

from Quite Frankly   (after Petrarch's *Canzoniere*)

1
if you can read the afterglow
of all the friction I connived in
escaping to the fairground so very young
& so variously insane
I hope you'll recognise a few shapes
if only by the state of the trellis
& that pain in the stomach
which is mainly knots in the convention
I don't blame them for crossing the street
when I come trudging down the contents page
I'd do it myself & head for the coconut shy
but it's long gone now & the hole hurts
the most intoxicating music of the fair at night
reduced to diesel & syringes

4
the universe explores its possibilities
whether you like it or not
nosing up every crack & atom
x+y making curry at 3 in the morning
you can have it for lunch in Hunstanton
with Italian wine & a yard of swiss roll
no-one's going back to work now
not with the Canaries two-nil down
you can understand why so many gods
chose the middle east instead of Norfolk
boiled the pot & kept chucking in chickens
& whatever anyone thinks they've learned
they still review their options
when they see her stroll past the bookies

7
anything of value has been banished
by a committee of the lazy
the greedy & the habitually thick
so where do we go from here?
these days it's hard to even see the stars
which once offered a perspective on our lives
now anyone dedicated to poetry
is awarded the status of freak
you only work for poetry & love?
do it in rags in that caravan then
& raise a glass of cold water to art
you'll walk this road alone my friend
you know that as well as I do
well it's too late to turn back now

11
I haven't seen your face unveiled
since you learned of my desire
sowing silence in the sky from which
my boomerang won't come back
as long as I was biting down on those
dreams which electrified my heart
I was free to see your sympathetic beauty
but then Cupid lifted the lid of my bin
your blond hair was hidden
away with your overwhelming eyes
my life-support system unplugged
I slump in this valley of the shadows
my heart beats my head feels like death
places a veil over the sight of you

from The Sardine Tree

next summer
a new work of art
will be prompted
on an August afternoon   think
in the broad depths   of a
of an old artichoke's   title
purple flower where
three bees sleep

www.ingramcontent.com/pod-product-compliance
Lightning Source LLC
Chambersburg PA
CBHW031150160426
43193CB00008B/314